MACMILLAN AND COMPANY LIMITED
Little Essex Street London WC2
also Bombay Calcutta Madras Melbourne

THE MACMILLAN COMPANY OF CANADA LIMITED
70 Bond Street Toronto 2

ST MARTIN' PRESS INC
175 Fifth Avenue New York NY 10010

PRINTED IN GREAT BRITAIN BY
THE BOWERING PRESS PLYMOUTH

The Lions' Mouths

Poems by Alan Brownjohn

LONDON
MACMILLAN
MELBOURNE · TORONTO
1 9 6 7

Contents

Acknowledgements

are due to the editors of the following, in which various of these poems first appeared:

Ambit

The Bulletin

Developmental Medicine and
    Child Neurology

Encounter

A Group Anthology

The Listener

The London Magazine

New Measure

The New York Times

The Paris Review

Peace News

The Spectator

Stand

The Times Literary Supplement

The Transatlantic Review

The Western Mail

A. B.

K. S. T.

The Situation

For it was that the cousins never came,
And so we could not know what they were like.
They never did walk out in their overwhelming way
To stand by the streaming water-butt, or
To hold the fence with their girls' adult hands.
This garden can't be remembered having them laughing,
So they remain a possibility:
That after our disappointment with man
And with dogs and with travel and with remaining still,
From our last armchairs we shall come to know
That there are the cousins left; who, that day,
Were to come, and did not, and are there to be tried yet.

Farmer's Point of View

I own certain acre-scraps of woodland, scattered
On undulating ground; enough to lie hidden in. So,

About three times a year, and usually August,
Pairs of people come to one or another patch. They stray

Around the edges first, plainly wanting some excuse
To go on in; then talking, as if not concerned,

And always of something else, not what they intend,
They find their way, by one or another approach,

To conducting sexual liaisons — on *my* land.
I've tried to be careful. I haven't mentioned 'love'

Or any idea of passion or consummation;
And I won't call them 'lovers' because I can't say

If they come from affection, or lust, or blackmail,
Or if what they do has any particular point

For either or both (and who can say what 'love' means?)
So what am I saying? I'd like to see people pondering

What unalterable acts they might be committing
When they step down, full of plans, from their trains or cars.

I am not just recording their tragic, or comic, emotions,
Or even the subtler hazards of owning land —

I am honestly concerned. I want to say, politely,
That I worry when I think what they're about:

I want them to explain themselves before they use my woods.

Reasons for Suspicion

They thought a sick flesh could begin
Of nothing but itself, since

Maggots were known to be
Created live by sun on meat.

What bred in silence, un–
Accountably could be most evil, so

A sexual dishonour looked
That sort of decay. Let her, then,

Not have walked in the sun.
Taint is so quiet; already

It could have started, each breast's
A suppurating disc of skin.

And they could argue: 'There's no
Dividing life from infection:

We are all out of some contagious lust.
Civilizations of refined

Bacteria (brave strains, rebuffing
Every drug) would doubtlessly

Claim and praise the great certitudes,
Would celebrate the awful

Mystery of self-engendering life.'

Poem on my Birthday

An open prospect to walk: miles of cloud this morning,
And no one else has chosen this way for a walk.
I am not too many years old yet, the body still responds
Quite easily. There is a sea wind
                        Pleasing even, and a fragile light
Good to stride in quickly. The world is neat and clear
— The clifftop distances —
And my eyes continue strong enough to see.

Footsteps just echo here closely: quick, blunt sounds.
Alone on a grey, paved stretch — to be walked
By crowds this afternoon — I jump alone to the beach
To chance the cold, and receive
                        The air and the mist, or spray
In a bloodless paleness on my uncovered hands.
And there is clean sand now, which gives and whitens
At the pressure of my shoes; flakes up, around.

Nothing is out at sea, the sea is wild.
But I can run, still run, up rough long blocks
Of stone, in stairs, where tide-grit lodges,
And in my compact self be a minor
                        Challenger of this weather
— Though under the top, dried surfaces of the pebbles
I notice the hidden sides are wet: salt stains
Blur the leather of my shoes.

Yet I walk, still, and look; having no fixed time
For being back — not even nightfall. If ships
Were to try this sea, they would need ample reasons;
And breakwaters, much though worn by water's rages,
                        Still profess a purpose
Larger than one might guess from their wear and waste.
I walk and look without an aim at all
Past their punctual gauntness. And I am wrong, I know,

But I could easily wish that I always walked
In this mood or place; having here gone back so far
On the particulars of definite emotion,
Or from the things I am required to feel.

                               There seems so much
Potentiality in a sunlight which promises, now,
Though it never will break out. I could not run two miles,
Which once I might have, nearly,

But I can think, from striding rapidly,
That I could, still. And I would see, in everything,
A sort of past expectancy, yet. It's the clarity
Of the bleak, bright air of the sea
                               Suggesting this
— Raising an energy nearly surprising me.
With it, I'll walk towards that bay and house,
Although the tide won't let me quite arrive.

Failure to Statue

My God, I have outwitted you now,
Who in my own lifetime, born after me,
My deskmate and my tyrant,

Ground me gradually down. I'll sit from
Every direction to gaze, any City Council
Seat to pay my ironies to your crazed

Posture on pocked granite horseback
In the typical dead centre of our park.
I'll be there to praise, of course. I'll wear my little hat

Like a cowed ordinary citizen's, my turned eyes
Rigid past and past your last, enormous,
Petrified salute, arm tethered stiffly in air

To your braided, stone field-marshal's cap.
I'll tender daily any begging bird
That stops by you where we voted you should ride

For ever (forgotten at least with respect),
And I'll do it because no one else will,
Because nobody else ever will.

The Suggestion

Consideration says you lose a moth by sliding a card
Under a quick glass shut on the wall patch where it sits
And carrying it out, perhaps to a light, to the midnight street.

I am saying to you, then, have understanding ready to devise
Your equivalent trick: get friends, have activities ready to
    divert me
Coming, unignorable and restless, to fret your neat room.

Where the ball ran into the bushes,
And I was sent to find it, being
Useful for that more than to play their game,
I saw instead
This badge, from someone's brother, in
Some regiment of that war: a trophy
Begged for and polished, coveted certainly,
But lost now, slightly touched with dust already,
Yet shining still, under smooth leaves drab with dust.
I knew that people prized such trophies then,
It was the way of all of us. I might,
For no one looked, have taken it
For mine. I valued it. It shone
For me as much as anyone.
And yet some fear or honesty, some sense
It wasn't to be mine — it wasn't more —
Said No to all of this. Besides,
They shouted in the distance for their ball.
For once quite quickly, I
Made up my mind
And left the thing behind.

Ode to Felix

At that tired eye-level point where
Impulse buying starts, he
Was there in flush, banked rows in
The supermarket: Felix the Cat.

Two dozen cat-food packets, patterned
For sales appeal, repeated two
Dozen static gestures of his face who
Almost first made cartoons animate.

I remembered that black-and-white
Stroll, brought back on the t.v. screen
About twenty years after: undoubtedly
Smart for its time, the commentator said.

Yes, he had all the possibilities
Already, little early Felix. His
Famous walk was even then the quaint, quick
Cartoon swagger, his features were

The easy prototype of all
Those smirking descendants, capering
In slick, flourished lines, richer
For the primary colours, and running on

Down and down a million celluloid frames
Hand-painted in endless studio rows by
Patient, paid artists reducing everything to
That clear-cut, lucid world, while

Elsewhere other grown men sound-tracked
The basic squawk. — This way was
The world infested by your
Charming animal kingdom, Felix, having

Driven out real beasts. Numberless
American children responded to
The uncle-funny voices, actually came
To look like Mickey Mouse. In the

Demure eyes of innumerable
Homely girls and wives lived
Bambi's primal innocence. Felix,
You were first of all those lovably

Blundering and resourceless dogs and
Elephants who helped to make our
Gross and failing natures bearable.
You set off Li'l Abner, firm and strait,

Shouldering over fields with no effort, as in
Our own fulfilment dreams, you
Tamed with Snow White all our dwarfs
And witches, you helped to paint

Donald Duck on the fuselage of
The bomber for Hiroshima. If today
A man in the *Sunday Times* Colour
Supplement makes t.v. commercials

To pay to make his very own cartoon
Satirizing agencies, the credit's
Partly yours, and you can be proud to think your
Walt Disney voted for Goldwater ...

I would not buy your food, I have no cat.
I can pass on down the stacked and shining
Aisles to other violences (the frozen red
Chops glossed in cellophane on puce, plastic trays)

But I'm not to pass without that sense, again,
Of one of my more elementary sorts of
Going mad: Your thousands of representatives,
Felix, walking into my world, writing my

Morning letters, modulating from the shapes
Of strangers outside the house, answering
My alarm calls for Fire, Police, *Ambulance*. In
That last nightmare trap and maze, they

Strut and chirp their obscene, unstoppable
Platitudes, Felix, while I run round and
Round and round to destroy their pert, joking smiles
And scream my own voice hoarse into their cute squeak.

A Difficulty

Moving across the light, on agitated hips,
She hurries away breadcrusts and grapestones
And glances in mid-talk, as if from fear,
At the irreproachable sea. Lanes frown away
Through the gaps in the hills she is looking at now
In the other window; but the floor throws up
Immediately, there, fresh patterns of her hands
And hair quite undismayed. So why is afternoon's easiness
Not beginning easily? Is the room
Not set correctly for the thing to come?
Or did we break some subject much too soon?

Trio

He has now gone with the toy gun into the greengrocer's shop
And is using some mock ploy with the greengrocer's girl.
She is cramped up, uncomfortably half-sat on the long ledge
Of the frozen food Cool Cabinet. She looks
A suitable imitation of absolute fright, she raises
Her hands and gives a visible but inaudible shout
— The traffic is so loud — as he gestures with the Xmas gun
Towards the celery or the till. She is a tall excitable
Girl of the kind wearing tinted, attenuated glasses
And patchy coloured nails. He is thick, blunt, overcoated
Wedge of a middle-class man with several parcels,
Including the toy gun. Now suddenly the proprietor, in a green
    coat,
Comes out of the store at the back and throws a horrified stare,
And shrinks himself, trembling, against the potatoes
In their brown, stolid banks. The man with the wooden red gun
Speaks, you can see, but you can't hear anything he says,
And all of them are standing in these postures still,
As they might be if the gorgon glance of a photographer
Had taken them all in flagrant tableau to present to the future:
On Xmas Eve, behind the green leaves and pink paper
Of the lighted trade window of 'Mackin's Best Fruit', between
Frozen plaice fillets and South African oranges.

The Preservation

It's quite worth keeping your surprise at the untrodden
Snow on the long step that particular winter night
— As if we had been indoors for days —

As in that time your every movement told,
And looked responsible. Never had your feet
Set out their marks on things with such grave care,

Or honour of any place. And all the mocking
Extensions to words in your hands' actions
Drained right away, or were absolved

In one cupped, simple gesture, collecting
(To taste and to smile) some snow in a quick mild heap
From the near top of the street wall.

By Paul's Kitchen Clock

He trembles, now, at his spyholes of jealousy. How
Appalling his guessing is! Not even a frost night
And white, hard grass such that their body-spaces would show
As hot, cleared blanks on the indifferent ground where they lay
— This would not have kept them back.
So, knowing what door they must surely re-enter by,
He waits to snatch on any audible step, guessing
Signs on her of hand-marks, in her freed and shaken hair,
And stands ready to be unable to overhear
Words whose meaning he will watch
On their lips, which smile them out; storing for just himself
All of these facts — as politicians learn to cherish
Each act of slander, planning their rivals' overset
With a decayed, set calmness, like the moon's.

A Hairdresser's

Something I remember from six is
Waiting for mother to dry, sat with
Home Chat and knitting books to read while
The warm cage glowed round her settled hair.

That was in a corner up in a
Room above the Gentlemen's Saloon,
Out of the way. But they *exhibit*
Them now, as here, turning magazines

Under the gesturing fingers of
Their talkative priestesses. Tall glass
In the High Street, florid with pot-plants,
Sets the new style: Huge, groomed photographs

And offers of 'Life restored'. It's a
'Fine art', you couldn't relate it to
Any usefulness; in this, having
Less of a function, even, than some

Oildom's backscratcher, following his
Chevrolet to the gaming tables
In a Super Snipe. I wish to feel
My complaint is better than a mere

Chafing memory of a child's hours
Waiting and waiting; it sees the point
With a cool rationality; it has
The courage to reject some things. . . .

But — 'If they want to', drones out some
Fool-libertarian voice, 'let them. Why
Shouldn't they do as they like?' (You
Have heard — or maybe used — that very tone!)

Passing in High Street rain, I repeat
My glance at that window and its line
Of faces locked in hives. No. I can't
Wish I were as liberal as that.

Skipping Rhyme

Pain of the leaf, one two —
Word of the stone, three, four —
Foot of the dark, pit of the hand,
Heart of the cloud, five, six, and
Out!

Skip.

Nora she had white eyes,
Mary she had black —
Helen looked in Grey Man's Wood and
Never came
Back!

Jump.

Nora draws a green thread,
Mary spins it blue —
But Helen will not bind it till her
True Love makes it
True!

Quick!

One, two, leaf of the pain,
Three, four, stone of the word,
Five, six, dark of the foot, hand of the pit,
Cloud of the heart, and
OUT!

Museum

I do not celebrate the birds in themselves:
They are prey-creatures, and the gloomy, the
Resinous eyes they had howl
Savagery and all marks of loathing yet.
I do not celebrate them even as pedestalled
Birds in well-dusted cases, in clear arrangement
With informative captions for the curious;
Though this will help the scholars much.
I celebrate them because you could be taking
Them into your own serene context, calming
The brusque beaks into a frivolous gentleness,
Disarming their fierce habitats and names
As unimportant things — if you were here.
A pity you are not. I would guess it
Not more than a few days now that you will have
Virginity to tame these carnal owls.

Class Incident from Graves

Wednesdays were guest night in the mess, when the colonel expected the married officers, who usually dined at home, to attend. The band played Gilbert and Sullivan music behind a curtain. . . . Afterwards the bandmaster was invited to the senior officers' table for his complimentary glass of Light or Vintage.
                                            (Good-bye to All That)

At the officers' table, for half an hour afterwards, port,
The bandmaster. He accepts, one drink long,
All the courtesy of the gentlemen. They are suave, and equal.
'I expect with your job . . . Do you find . . . Oh well. . . .'
The bandmaster edges the shining inch of port along the grain
    of the table,
Precisely covering one knot with the transparent
Base of the glass. He crouches forward over the polished wood
Towards the officers, not comfortably convivial,
Eyes always going to the face speaking next,
Deferential, very pleased.
The band put away their instruments out at the back, having
Drunk their beers, standing.
The detachable pieces of brass lie down
In the felt grooves of the cases, just as they should.
Nine-thirty strikes.
There is laughter of men together, coming from inside.
'Mitchell's still in there, hob-nobbing with the officers.'

The Balcony

There isn't really telling what she stands from,
And why her back leans over, and her head
Is down on her hands, white-gripped on the rail.

Whether from fright, or grief, or stubbornness,
Or whether she cries, or only ponders
The mesmerizing height she gazes on
With a most tired concentration: none of this
Is reasonable to guess. Even when

She lifts her thrown-down glance, face-flushed, I can't
Tell more about why it is, because she has now
Done what I hoped against, turned her head, away.

Eight Investigations

a junction

Not to meet, then. But can't we maintain
One concessionary contact: of
Some meeting in theory — for instance,
Making an agreement to retain
A *kind* of connection by a glance
Each day at some same landmark? Or have

An intersection of routes planned out
On journeys we are often making?
This could be a place where we again
— At quite different times! — could no doubt
'Meet'; (I would cross it like a night train
Crossing points — rapid, darkened, trembling.)

Sprogo (in the Great Belt)

In that sea-stretch, one minor island,
It makes a misty scrap of jutting
Land from wide water. A calmer green
Covers, though, all but one nearly hand-
Wise gesture of cliff, where can be seen
A caged, rusted lantern, cautioning.

You could be compared with any slim,
Chill, passing thing, at will. Yet, the same,
Let me let this dwindling seamark make
Another image: as, on a whim,
Such a quick distant shape could quite take
The diminuendo of your name.

her drawing

No, this Snow Queen (or Cordelia)
Lies drawn, for you, quite differently;
Is merely some unthinking release
Of a moment's work. Still, I see her
As a projection from your own face,
And think: not knowing, you let her be

Like some taller screen image of your
Own contained precision (thus that high
Glance, your own, muting the hands' gestures).
But as she is yours, I must feel
She is truth itself, all such features
Thrown that large by some flattering eye.

second drawing

A kind of swirl of bracken where curve,
Though static, somewhat ambiguous
Symbols, as if grown part of that ground
Of black-stressed, intricate roots (these leave
The surface at no point, but twist round
And upwards into the dubious

Branches of the plant, form letters, signs
Which could mean your name: such as now bring
My mind quite out, away from this sheet,
Elsewhere in time; past these pencilled lines
To their sudden, living start: your neat
Intent smile, your tensed fingers moving).

concession

Privileged now to see you, tell me
(Because I can't know whether I stare
On some frank, actual thing, that skin
Utterly real, or if I yet see
Only a surface which locks me in
With protective, invisible care

As when one looks out at things through glass)
— Are you like somewhere known with plain sight,
Just as clear as you seem? Or do you
Screen off real knowledge, so letting pass
Everything but the quickest key to
That country of air, your clean daylight?

distance

Invent two rings of falling light; wide
For you in the south and the sun's rage,
But not my light — obliged on a neat
Metal table surface to refer
Only to the black words on this sheet:
Chilled, northern light, bronze-shaded. One page

Written already, lies just outside,
In the fawn dusk of the table-edge,
A failure. Still; I can't stop. Be sure
A thousand mere dark miles won't divide
Fact from longing, break down this posture
Of vain love to a better knowledge.

cliffs

Merely thinking up your name in this
Hazardous high strip and ledge in air
Works a consolation: simply that,
Repeating you, any daring is
Practically possible — leant flat
On this shuddering wall, I can stare

Down on the mapped rocks, or out to sea
Unfrightened. Yet in some safe room to
Hear those syllables. . . . The difference
Scares and drowns out all talking for me.
There is no quick courage helps with this
Unexpected way of meeting you.

epistemology

My same eyes once jumped through the page-long
Paragraphs, flickering over such
Banks of abstract words! A *physical*
Power those words had, that caught the strong
Breath of the mind away. The real
Equivalent, now, is your face. Much

That same way your eyes glance this as mine
Glanced; which now face to your forehead's small
Shades and meanings, seek to sublime this
Craving in verbal charts, and refine
Its enigma in a healing verse:
Neurotic; and metaphysical.

Pimm's Cat

if less naive,
would be more animal,
would scrabble with
fierce candour at the door,
or set snow tracks
to purposeful places;

but (for the law
of average's sake)
there should be still
such creatures as he is:
uncontrolled, mild,
shabby, not zealous, a

good redress for
too many of the sort
whom the hard praise
of the practical tongues
sets in a beast's
requisite infamy.

The Shadow

It is that, unconsciously, you
Stop short of the harsh, crude edges
Of the obvious symbols. Your

Discrimination of purpose
Is plain in your least conscious acts;
Allowing the occurrence of,

For example, this shadow. Though
The door, only half open, keeps
The real truth of you for inside,

One patch of the nearer white wall,
By which you sit, takes — not your black
Shadow from strong light straight on you

But — a blurred, vague shape from the light
Diffused throughout the room; no sharp
Cave-shadow (some mere copy) but

Just this implication of shade
On the wall. Discrimination
Of purpose reduces this tint

To less than less than a symbol,
To the least intimation of
Your self; and here, as in all ways,

By which (though sensible to a
Rough touch) you would reserve yourself,
You are quick, solemn and discreet.

Office Party

We were throwing out small-talk
On the smoke-weary air,
When the girl with the squeaker
Came passing each chair.

She was wearing a white dress,
Her paper-hat was a blue
Crown with a red tassel,
And to every man who

Glanced up at her, she leant over
And blew down the hole,
So the squeaker inflated
And began to unroll.

She stopped them all talking
With this trickery,
And she didn't leave out anyone
Until she came to me.

I looked up and she met me
With a half-teasing eye
And she took a mild breath and
Went carefully by,

And with cold concentration
To the next man she went,
And squawked out the instrument
To its fullest extent.

And whether she passed me
Thinking that it would show
Too much favour to mock me
I never did know —

Or whether her withholding
Was her cruelty,
And it was that she despised me,
I couldn't quite see —

So it could have been discretion,
And it could have been disgust,
But it was quite unequivocal,
And suffer it I must:

All I know was: she passed me,
Which I did not expect
— And I'd never so craved for
Some crude disrespect.

Message for the Time of Year

Filling the tape-end, a girl's voice
Was saying: Summer spreads us, we
Are vagrant. The whole light season
Seems only a hive of seething conténts:
Lacklands get land, -loves love,
The pen-friends whore here after our language,
Madeleine, Claude, Yvette. We learn
To want flower-dresses, and to disobey.

Matutinal

Strong sleep alone in the house makes all the difference.
It must be a good dull day, though: and no birdsong.
Then sleep enough will set most issues right.

So will the indulgent water of the bath,
Where I lie next, ten reassuring minutes. This
Can render any problem easy, and

I often take a pad in, for jotting solutions,
Putting it with the soap and the torn sponge
On the bath edge; it might be useful.

So it's ten-thirty, and everything is easy
— But now a brash sunlight points out patterns
Of undying dust in air to think about,

Or takes up the steam from the surface of the water
Like rising, drifting smoke. And secondly,
The telephone is arrogantly ringing. There is

Time just for the towel, and to leap downstairs
Past the impending shadow of someone
About to knock at the locked and bolted door.

I have snatched off the receiver of the phone, yet
The thing keeps somehow ringing and ringing.
A fault on the line somewhere? As if I would know!

My sleep was worthless: the caller fidgets and coughs
On the step outside; the phone rings on; the black
Receiver slithers on my sweating ear.

The Victory

I think it's yours. Furrowing the
Sweat-nights groping for metaphors
— Like the bed's cool patches —
It was hope even then. And other fluences

Carried me somewhere: as, telepathy:
Winging blind wires to carry somehow
News to you. Mad, but it all allowed
The thing to continue. Now, though,

The wires are down. My brain can't ever seem
To stop still enough to think you. My
Bland words talk alone about themselves.
It's yours, this victory, then,

By simple waiting. And, if only you
Might find just what you truly wish through
That same patience — building where
You use it now to reap such disrepair.

Diana and the Transmitter

Being below it, well!
There are no words at first.
There is nothing quite like
This bloody great steel tower,

Which won't be a toy,
Or any brick, sensible thing,
But coerces the feeble eye
Up hair-thin ladders

To nominal platforms, thrown
From windy leg to leg
— Where it leaves it, hurt and scared,
To acquire a disturbing thought:

If by any crude, romantic
Ruse of some enemy
I had either to climb that stair
Or never see her again

— To climb to the spiked top,
Or even some lower stage
(And I dread this so much
It's almost probable!) —

I know that I couldn't climb,
Not even for that sake;
And I am so humbled by
Those with heads for heights

Or knowledge of engineering, that
I refuge in defiance,
And uncomfortably strike some right
Attitudes, out of fear; like these:

I rebuke the brisk graduates
Working for this tower
(Reforming, transforming
The medium from inside!)

I reject the proponents of better
Advertising art (those makers
Of terylene haloes for whores)
And the conscience-salvers with Granada.

I will not take the excuses
Of the inexcusables who
Make the animal voices
For cartoons; for whom

This tranquillizing monument
Seems particularly built. And
I question the final moral right
Of this meccano phallus

To landscape, anyway, here.
I'd ask this of Collins,
Orr Stanley, Simms; and would have
Their answers less than smooth.

And look: this is nearly making up
For any earlier lack, out
Of weakness, of any proved love
— If, as I think, these curses

Are gesturing to defend (for want
Of any daring will of mine
To try to climb the thing) her
Every facet of virginity.

The Wall

Sunlight goes on making
And making its reappearances on that stained wall
Without alteration. It's getting
More elderly, I would say; goes a mellower course
Over chair-dent and sweat-mark,
Moving a window-square which seems
Not so clear now at the edges. To have
Sat once among such motes and specks
Was to be glad to see dust made quick
By illumination, interruption by liveliness.
This dust now is literal dust, shown up
By this changed also sun as wandering in air
As thinking wanders in the aged — with
An unkind pleasantness. Such sun
Used not to calm me near to sleep like this.

At the Time

Perhaps the daring made it
Seem all right. Or
The memory of the daring.
At the time, there were
The midges, was the fidgeting
Of bottles in someone's
Crates; all the mere
Ungainliness of limbs:
There was the wanting
To get it done and over,
And to resume a proper,
Acceptable posture.
Only much afterwards, was there
The having done, was there
That person (think of it),
And that place; all the daring
Shame of it. Only afterwards,
That. There was, really,
Nothing at all of this,
Nothing at all, at the time.

Apology for Blasphemy

I can formulate two
Excuses in mitigation:
First, blasphemy surely admits
Some firm, good name:

Only the loved names can
Incite to abuse and treasons:
You cannot blaspheme over what
You must despise.

Second it was, of course,
A trick, in assistance of love,
And no truth. This is the plain fact.
To please a spy,

Huge factories are built
With shuddering walls of dark steel
— Shells of deception, all a lie.
My words did that.

Let an amending tongue
Now penitently cast for means
To rebegin flattery, since
I shrink in fear

Of how I have blasphemed
If nothing can be seen to crack
These literal words; unmake
What they imply.

It is with metaphor
We can assuage, abolish and
Create. I will apologize
With metaphors:

Listen: you could not know,
But when the snow dashed your face, it made
Patterns on white, violent glass, stone-
Scattered; and as

Your mouth just opened, now,
In a slight surprise, all the lions'
Mouths on the bronze financial doors
Dropped their gripped rings.

Affinity

He. This thing we have, one means by it what starts
   Between two people not near to one another
   Who have hardly met and never spoken,
   Yet know some faint intangible linking
   — Neither to be made firm, nor yet to be broken.

She. I don't see it like this at all, but
   In opposites: a sudden image of this woman,
   Myself, set off on this dark road unaccompanied,
   Pacing between blank hedges, her feet
   Leaving and reaching echoes, behind and ahead,

   And all at once this new thing arriving,
   The darkness thinning and varying, the car
   Rushing the channels of her ear, its light
   Climbing the sides of trees. And her one doubt is to
   Ask what *kind* of man he is at the wheel that night

   (Is he lover, enemy, casual messenger,
   To give all her landscape that white leaping look?)
   Since although she cowers back in the mist, bent
   In self-protecting fear of what he means,
   She has called and craved for . . . this new element.

Nasty Habit

The sky is so white, the paper is so white.
The unattended leaves of January lie in the damp.
The girl who ran upstairs wrote
Her face, pausing, on the blank of the white wall
(Or on my eyes) with black and pointed hair.
That clock is very fast, the time exists.

And, well, the emotional components exist
For something; for one of the three or four
Attempts at answering 'loneliness'.
Here is a chair comfortable for meditation,
Arms long enough to stretch on, back facing
Towards the window and concealing any

Thought or action I might have or take.
It's up to me. I can sense the moral framework
Even now expanding to allow
A lot of things. Virtually every gesture
Takes on its altruistic look, and
'I had to do it . . .' feels an honourably

Far-off last resort. . . . So I start to write.

No Good

It is no good if any man dreams
Her love is attainable by schemes:
No one can win these modern wars,
Why squander tactics on this sort of cause?

It is no good if one decides
Love can be bought, extravagance provides:
She will be right to stay unmoved,
Those won those ways may end unloved.

It is no good if, slyly, one defends
Courses her other lover recommends:
Guile with her is out of place,
She can read any hidden face.

It is no good in the rare state
Of abused purity, the discarnate:
She will think stories, and surmise;
Agree, with pity in her eyes.

It is no good pretending your
Passion is an unbreakable law:
She may obey it! You'll be spent
In some obscene predicament.

It is no good any way one takes,
The sin is travel if roads are mistakes,
The plague is feet if it's no good proceeding:
I do not think this is too misleading.

Warm People

Where complete light is so
narrow it lasts — for six
weeks — all the twenty-four
hours, it's obvious that
window ledges should fill
with tentacle creepers,
or freak geraniums
should front the Arctic with
some days' brash petals. . . .

                              But
I would need it explained
why, where eight months of
the fecund calendar
flowers crowd the out-of-doors,
people still nurse blooms for
their cramped houses, lodge them
in pots and boxes round
every piled room (while
leaves cram the windows up
outside.) Is there a point
in their insistence on
this claustrophobia
of growth?

                    It wouldn't be
their claim to one success?

A Few Syllabics

You said you couldn't
Do other. You were
That conventional
You just walked 'into
The night.' It hurled rain.

They had left on the
Light in the builders'
Yard to stop burglars,
And you had eight wet
Miles' ride. But what was

Not usual was (and
I didn't know) you
Carried a man's child
Two months uninter-
rupted away in

You. It wasn't mine,
I loved you, and by
This bit of chance, your
Not telling me, you
Left, to take her on

Till birth, and to push
Her onwards down time
To stand here (a child
Two months in her too,
Which I do know, and

The new child not mine
Either) where the light
Left on in that yard
Again shows me that
Shape I love, as we

Look at your photo
She holds (bit of chance!)
And I wonder if,
After all these dark
Things, I'll let *her* leave.

Incident in Milan

They are going about it now
In such silence; yes,
In the garden even:
Bringing to its end
By mutual disagreement
Their long, long liaison
— The line-clothed girl
And the Italian, Maurielli.

Such a long drag of
Time were they united,
By their only difference:
Of sex; in all else
Being the same, two
Mere stones of dullness,
Solidly grating
Surfaces in talk, talk.

She would elbow
Past him in the kitchen,
And resent the obtruding
Angle of his chair;
She might push his hair
Accidentally out of
The neatness he once
Contrived for her

And then, from habit, kept (he
Hating her, truly,
For that, and glaring
Back to her trim food
— Insulting in the
Gourmet's care with which
She set it out, between . . .)
The violences of

These inarticulates,
Their moments of hounding truth,
Have no Method dignity,
Really. Are more like
Abandoned sandflats where
No one lives, or ploughs.
Close your own shutters. Read
Or sleep. Let them alone.

Yesterday's Fire

One lifting tatter of black, burnt paper
Soared up, and stayed, like a raven watching,
On a tree's limb. But I am not deterred
By would-be omens.
                              A hand quite over
A hand, but quietly, is the only start,
And to part her fingers wrong. Properly so
I placed my left hand then.
                              You must be sure
You don't impose some will that gentleness,
Not wanting to offend, might not resist.
I said, I said this carefully,
                              'You may withdraw
Your hand mine holds on if you really wish.'
Just then, a brash wind switching the drifting
Of the smoke our way, we both at once
                              Jumped back,
Hands kept together; and she did not quite
Disengage till the thing I said
Could be fully taken in. But she understood.
                              'You must take back
The hand yourself. I do not want to give
You back discourtesies.' And nicely smiled,
'Make it your will — please not my petulance.'
                              And as I brought

My hand away, I glanced into the tree,
Where, as I looked, I saw that tatter fall,
Which may have made an omen after all.

God's Creatures

We all hate the sturdy nobility
Of the horse, we mock at it in cartoons
And carnivals. Such set, single-minded
Devotion we parody most with the
Two halves of the pantomime animal,
At odds which way to lurch.

                                Somewhere I once
Saw a pseudo-horse climb up to the high
Diving board at a big swimming gala,
Hesitate on the edge, unfunnily,
Then slough off to become two boring frogs
Which grossly flopped through the chlorinated
Air into the water while we watched,
And indulged in human play at the deep end.

Sunsets

Suddenly caught by how it seems
Possible and quite credible that,
In this last windless minute at

Sunset, that downspread of fields I watch
(Gazing past, from this vantage hill,
Just visible cows to the town) will

Have darkened a little — even though
You can't measure this, and it may be
Your eyes don't tell it truthfully —

I sense a comparison with
Some points in the progress of love:
Times when each element *has* to move

At just the stage when you would want
It at rest — when, dispassionate
-ly, you would want to define and state

To yourself just where you stand. It may
Be a simple error to believe
That love runs on like that, you can deceive

Yourself quite easily. But
So often love seems to be set
On rushing you past anywhere you get

A chance to arrest it, and talk.
And in this, as with nightfall, you sense
That you cannot make much pretence

Of defying any darkness.
It leaves you no other choice.
It happens in front of your eyes.

A Sunday Breakdown

Crossing the coarse pebbles with scrupulous tread, in
His Gracechurch Street clothes, poor Ludbrook
Goes out on that long jutting wall to the end point
— Where, evilly foamless and smooth, the sea
Lurches over it — and sits down with his *Times*
Where it's three inches deep, and puts his umbrella up

And waits (reading the Court Circular and Birthdays Today)
For the police, or the lifeboatmen, or the Civil Defence
To be the first to come and argue that what
He does is irrational or dangerous,
And would he stop because he ceases to amuse,
And he is driving away the custom from the place.

The Lost Surprise

Your dog I hate strains from you and would run.
A dead-leaf dust confirms the arid grass.
My eyes, faint from newsprint, watch some odd man
Prowl round and round in a feigned casualness
— Voyeur, today, of different lovers. How
Could we two serve such curious interests now?

And yet I think you brought the dog in case:
He was your good excuse, lest I should move.
Not that he would protect, but just increase,
By simply sitting there, your chance to have
Some breaking sentence said: he could run loose
At any tiresome moment you might choose.

I have to relish, though, this flattery
You build for both of us; that dares to claim
That lost surprise you need for you to be
My main quest still, the reason that I came;
And brings this dog out on our autumn day
Squatting its aged cunning in the way.

In Crystal Palace Park

One January day, among full frail light:
The new stadium shut in blessed silence; sun,
Of the mild midwinter, glossing the gorilla's haunches;
The lake-sheet above the refreshment-room staying
Quiet, through the trees, as the Consort's white elk facing it.

But slumped and crooked at coffee, I think: Only
Beings like these trees can renew. Teachers or foresters
Could point out endless ring on new ring of survival;
Rafters are told of, whining in sympathy with storms;
Gateposts have launched unearthly leaves; and our Commission's

Dense, patterned groves elsewhere grow for when we are all dead.
Trees outlast us. Seasons — how many have *we?* — make no
    difference
To them, through centuries of vegetable time. — Yet use
Your human reason. Should we feel outfaced by even
These mere park glades, in all their bareness now?

At these moments of disquiet, take any single
Individual tree: your face (you can feel the grooved bark on)
Can almost defy it: for after ten years you can
Think its wear equalling yours. Even the inexpert eye
Can spot decay (like your own: each sad spring bravery of leaves

Seems like the brashness of rejuvenation drugs.)
And then you, councillors, murderers, can ride over
A Preservation Order; or citizen, set your crudest pedigree dogs
To do their natural work at some one tree. It surely was
As abstract 'trees' they had that lasting look.

— It's late. I leave the coffee cup, and step out warily
To the mild air again. Away from gulls, many separately
Walking the grass as one to some unattained place,
I hunch, and stride downhill. And pass each tree,
Not blessed with human reason, living its sober term.

The Space

Then why see it? This 'flat and ample
Space over which you walk at no one angle,
Led as by something very like your will?'

*You could go on with proper concerns. You
Are boiling tea, typing some letter, listening
To politics when it comes. Why let it, why let*

It come? — That pale, clean stretch
Stays small, and won't usurp the whole. So
I let it come. There is no harmful freedom.

*But where do you go across that space? Do you
See things, see anyone?* I don't go anywhere
But across it; taut and clear, though the wind leans at me.

Further, it might be a world, and not safe:
It might be stayed in. I keep it unfulfilled.
Its colour? Certain shadows, shades of green.

— And whoever she who walks there, and stands,
She won't tremble into definition, isn't
Like Fournier's girl, say, on the steps and real.

Then why let it come at all? Only, that to this
All common facts yearn to approximate,
While time strains to reach it. And it

Won't be otherwise, it refuses, and must
Return as plainly as before; nothing but
A kind of sober walking-space. — I see

You are not answered why, nor sense why I let it come.